Domestic Yoga

D1607713

Also by Jack Christian

Family System (2012)

Domestic Yoga

Jack Christian

groundhog
POETRY PRESS

2016

Library of Congress control number: 2016944899

ISBN: 978-0-9976766-1-7

Printed in the United States

Published by
Groundhog Poetry Press LLC
6915 Ardmore Drive
Roanoke, Virginia 24019-4403
www.groundhogpoetrypress.com

The groundhog logo is the registered trademark ™ of Groundhog
Poetry Press LLC

For Lucinda

Contents

The unexamined life's no different from

                  the examined life—

        - Charles Wright

The Next Life

I'd like in the next life to have most of the same attributes
but a better draw of blood genetics.
I'd upgrade to the Infiniti or Acura
from where I am with my Toyota
and put forth a more rational, cogent policy re: sun-tanning.
My sense of humor would appear as a man in the woods
beckoning.

All my noises sound like sighs.
This according to my wife.
And they sure do sound like sighing
when she plays them back from her mouth
in the tacit mirroring couples adopt.
We sit at the table in front of the woodstove
with our laptop monitors barely touching.

The Cloud

Oh, The Things You'll Put Yourself In
is what they read us,
and gave us all commemorative Whirlpools,
emblazoned Class of '96
and the valedictorian's, hers was a centrifuge.

But that was prep school,
Montpelier, Vermont, the one Frank M.
penned fictional memoir about,
and did occasionally attend
its carbuncular halls and thatches.

Now, they can all forget themselves…

What I want to talk about is how even keel I feel
sitting between the houseplants Spidey and Guy Spidey.

Who cares the nasturtium died?
The pickle plant returned—we thought it dead—
and I sowed the whole balcony with rosemary,
went inside, did this image search:

There's the Rhine like a parking lot…
Isle of Skye and it's gleaming…
and a thoughtful man-pushing-lawnmower
at magic hour on the album cover
of the band we liked way back
liked for their 10 or 12 minute songs,

for how in their dust beam

we could fade and fade out…

Yeah, it was kind of like that, omnipresent,
or by extension…
but when you consider the photo taken from above by helicopter
you know again this narrative of surveillance.

The Good Presbyterians

At night as a child
I put on my sleepwalking pants.

I made a sound my cohort could hear
and knew to follow.

These were our sleep vacations.
Receipts proved we went sleep-shopping.

In prayers we laid Tuesday gently over Sunday.
We couldn't be hurried.

We were hucksters in the final pew,
with our dads who also stayed awake.

They warmed milk. They drew baths.

They watched the late late late late
late late late late late late late show.

Blue Bayou

Maybe there's no choice
and my uncle's funeral
is your sister's wedding?

As always we reach the argument
and of course there's no argument

as in that direction the game repeats
and in this one
wrongly we think this life would be easy if we'd let it.

I guess I can buy the coincidence of his passing,
but what feels fated is never seeing him again—

the blank longer than intended. And still,

a certain pastel of mourning
a place still reserved for crying, for stillness

for the illusion of movement in his red blazer
even though he held on so long, too long,

and seeing him alive was sadder.

Poem in Film

This cocktail you sniffed cost 12 bucks
but did make you clairvoyant on your birthday.

We sure were sure, weren't we,
your new girl would fall for you
if you could cajole her into purchase
of that great in-town apartment
in the heart of Boys Town.

I'm sorry things fell apart
at the Christmas talk with her mother
and her mother's general weepiness
and the long-dead dad who died beside a football.

I'd like to know: at what opportunity
        at what crossroads, at what fractal life-crisis point,
        at what soul-fracking, at what gleaning of soul sands,
        at what intra-corpus irrigation, at what headtop removal,
        at what hidden arterial explosion,
        does one begin to describe himself as a spelunker?

If I was wrong when
surprise, surprise
turned out they had my passport behind the counter the whole time. . .

If something languished on visits made in gray, Champion sweatpants. . .

If purchasing the black pumpkin stout

on sale for the new holiday
was sign of a larger internal caterwaul…

> But all that is the plotting of a rust-belt sun-glint weep-eyed dream-cast
> sentimental, reform video…

The guy at the Petco puppy class where my Patty excelled
said his was a Dixie Dog – Nikita – rescued from a Kentucky ditch
outside a house-o-fire.

              If I did it in ignominy, if in subtle miscalculation of my own
health…well then.

Noons we spent trilling our R's at Amethyst Brook.
Evenings of the tv nudgings.

Evenings after that:
80 minutes college basketball,
one part 2%, three parts frozen yogurt,
plus a bowl
and spoon set
earned through our engagement.

I was 19
and all the nurse-practitioner wanted
was to tell me about chlamydia.

I beg your pardon
I'm something of a chronicler.

What's good about it
is when it becomes obsessional,

when I can lay it down
in this great non-narrative movie I make

called Life in In-Between Gestures.

I'm making it even now
with my pirated copy of Final Cut Pro, biorhythmic edition.

Homeopathy

We're lucky
to have a group that meets Thursdays

down the street,
and remedial help if necessary,

and extended-training-facilities access-passes,
and anti-parking-maleficence strategies

at the walk-in cessation tent
where also they sell apples for nominal sums,

and an infusion called Larchmont,
and a brochure for a place called Larchmont,

which, if you want, you can visit—
get gathered near the monastic life,

find out about the tea—how it's culled,
what thoughts concocted it.

I've been.

The Second Time I Fell in Love

When dogs kiss
it's because they've got the end of the same noodle
in their mouths.

When people kiss they want to breathe each other's breath.

They don't admit it.
Instead, they whisper bright things in the dark.
That's what they're doing on the stoop,
on the couch.

They think they can see each other's auras
but they haven't gotten enough rest.
They talk about drinking bathwater
and sucking rot from fingernails.

They don't care they don't mean it.

The second time I fell in love
it caused a snowstorm on the coast of Virginia.
I drove carefully and let the car get stuck.

We waited until two in the morning
and then we were thinking we could live
unbored in the world as peaceniks
that we could sleep inside the same shirt

that the weather was another kind of thought
that had ahold of us and wouldn't close.

The Beach

We had a branch and strolled out on it,
and it being antiquated
gave a different give,
the feeling of which we fastened with a thumbtack.

That was no way to start,
board beside anthropomorphized board
in the den with wood paneling…

I was a souvenir you found in the shop behind the shop.

When you felt you had to buy something, I was it—
a little mush-mouthed to imply my nonchalance
more sunny on a novel day,
as art invades where pattern is subverted.

Then, the videographer popped up to sue you—
that great curmudgeon of the dunes,
more nuanced when the day was cool.

You couldn't even buy this guy a burrito,
his pocket wizened by an old sparkplug or something—

as always our favorite rebellion into scrupulousness.
Big curtain we disdain to see.

And from where this passed-down stoical countenance?

A UFO

I thought I saw a UFO
cavort between the town dump
and our faux-Mexican eatery.

Was pretty sure about that,
but reports put it now as a C-5
over the Connecticut,

which is why I'm so suspicious of their knowledge.

First it was a saucer,
then it was a pizza slice,
now they're saying Maybe No Snow at All.

A Memory

The planned forest is no way out,
only options,
and still a little nonsense to dimple the order,

and the trail that takes us there
by a copse of cars,
as if once they formed a headlight circle

and are now a rusty installation
or more simply some patterned junk
that helps predict the seasons,

the ridge above like a crooked back,
before the campsite on the creek's little finger
with Meagan, Emma and Phil in warmest March,

as if we played some psychic role in the heat,
my hand-me-down Buick
full with wilderness gadgets.

It really was just that once —
on a rock in the river treading happily
against looming departure,

which could all be comparison to something else
but is just the memory, untimed,
the fire, the coals, and after —

a bit of gut pushing up through the muscle wall.
Is that a way to say it?

Unactionable Intelligence

What's the point stringing thoughts along
when it's true enough to have just none?

You're something else as the dusk arrives—
a further bouquet of knowing,
these first, then our better gestures
blown up with the gutter leaves,
red-faced as always and that's ok—
secret beer inside your cup.

Upon our return, our seats were gone,
our coats intact,
the both of us glad to celebrate the loss.
Later, at home, I thought to celebrate some death.
But that was just me misfiring,
and when I awoke
true love had rubbed me up
and named me "Technology Coordinator."

For a moment, I was a blinking hub
surrounded by the little lights
of a system in need of managing.

A blue marble wobbled through.

A Song

I'm the poet of French fries and beer gut.

Following the sidewalk I gather clues left by my psychologist.
Stepping out to take a call I find I'm locked on a small balcony.
Calmer now but still unable to accept these bogus pet fees.

At home enamored of a series of steps leading near my credit report.
I check the weather as if watchdog of the forecasters.
My bar-mate turns to me and says, "Brace Yourself, Honey."

Whoever argues for transcendence is owed beer by me.

In a white room I'm belching your favorite song.
I'm seeking divorce again
in a program meant to quash my fear of divorce.
The college kids are tanning on their roofs
and I admire their effort because roof-tanning seems uncomfortable.

Whoever stakes a position and defends it;
whoever ascribes to changeable reality,
nosing studiously toward truth, wearing truth like his nose—
I owe a beer.

At the mailbox awaiting a keyboard condom
because in three months I've thrice spilled beer on my keyboard.
I awake and realize tag sales are self-serious yard sales in essence.

These glowsticks inform my practice.
This 3 a.m. furniture moving is to accommodate you.
If your son is getting married, recruit me—
I've corralled many bridegrooms when they've sought to vamoose.

The hawks are in residence this month above the interstate.

Jobless still, I go about conferring beers
and stapling white bikes to street signs.

Worrying over everything and assuming nothing,
I proceed not unlike a baseball game.

Where was it one first learned words don't mean anything?

The dog and I form a man-dog combo and eat potato chips hilariously.

Whoever offers conspicuous thanks
without a hint of self-congratulation is owed a beer by me.

Whoever is more excited than the show of his excitement I owe a beer.

Has the man who's covered his car in bumper stickers
steeled himself with morning beers?

I've counted each dimple in the drop ceiling.

A bicycle appears on a tree in my yard
and I leave a somewhat friendly note requesting its removal.

You're the Maestro I'm the Minstrel

I wanted to be a smorgasbord of erotic discourse,
a sentence running skew to all its logics,
my one job to button up and get magnanimous,
every yawn some kind of artisanal service.

We held a sitcom intervention whenever you showed up.
You small fort of unnamable generosity, never a full-stop.
You, the small god of a compartmentalized trouble factory.
I mean, who writes an ode to an onion?

Two Guests Continued Talking

One had an idea and the other was willing to try it.

One had a hunch and an assumption,
the other thought both were worth a shot.

He had an energy you could hardly harness.
The other prided himself on being open to most things.

He was an idea man. They both were idea men.

Then, they were the upshot of an old conversation.
Then, they were fat old donkeys.

They were chewing the fat;
they were chewing each other.

They listed aphorisms pertaining to chickens.
One said, "Chicken sandwiches."

Their comedy was mostly situational
but still forthright enough to be redeeming.

Mother of Sadness

The Lord's Prayer echoes from the outdoor speaker
at the Mother of Sadness School.

It's raining and the students are all inside.

The words bounce off the mill buildings and come back,
as if the prayer were for the neighborhood.

It's Tuesday.
The school where I teach is pretending it's Monday.

Pretense is practice sometimes, I guess.
I say the prayer under the guise of remembering the words.

The voice moves directly into Hail Mary.

The voice seems ready to graduate
into announcing flight delays.

Funny that in a decade some kids will speak fondly
of their time at the Mother of Sadness.

I hope the school prepares them not to believe anything.

Had it been my school, at least the wet of my eyes
I could've expected.

What's it look like to be a rascal at the Mother of Sadness?

I kind of like this service blared to no one.

Does it happen only on Tuesdays I pretend are Mondays?

I imagine myself repentant of my own ambivalences.

There's an old park behind the school.
I could picture it transmogrified.

Particularities

But that's just summation of the sunny splendor,
this dogleg at Dragon's Tooth

when you expected chrysanthemums on the right,
as in the yolk a sacrilege to spoil the outer egg.

Really, it's an irrational grief response,
a subtler strategy for avoiding gab—

to be here, concocted so variously against arrival.

Well, I found the fence the forest hides
then counts amongst its realest density.

The Gift Economy

This is the tapping a foot will do in a trace of snow,
I said to bring you close.

I feel at times the shrill compulsion
that names us Fellow Travelers
only to lose the thread…
The collective mitten gets unstitched,
returns us to the apartment lawn,
weather advisories to keep things interesting.

And still, imagination persists, so much easier than invention—
on the post road smeared with pumpkin
or anyplace we might tag along,
such as an impromptu nature preserve,
beleaguered by property rights
but believed by a small populace,
laminate, paper signs making it so…

Neighbor, Ignore Me, but Please Trek Thru!

I'd say it happened just when we stopped being afraid for a nanosecond
and thought how pretty that'd be if we let it—
how immediate, how reassuring
as if to reconstitute bits of these affairs
by adding proper water.

Not even in pursuit of Mt. Lafayette,

just some minor peak.

Like, what if we could enjoy the particulate matter

    in this particular sunset,
    then switch on a giant magnet
    that sucked out the gunk?

Blackberry, Blackberry, Blackberry

After a good rain the quad becomes a slip-n-slide,
and even irreverence reforms into reverence.

I saw it up again early Tuesday
behind the tree splits
in *black sweet blood mouthfuls*
that fluttered off
to what I was about to think,
my own private Super Bowl.

The whole to appreciate
being everything and unafraid,
and with no idea but to inject our love
with what's good enough.
Then, hoo boy the roundness in your belly
greeted in our staunchest gibbers.

Now look at me,
supreme carpooler with everybody.

Bus Tour for the Holiday

So long flower pot.

I'd say try as far as you can untucked,
then grab an arm and complete the loop.

—as if that would work.

Or, in another iteration
throw pawpaws to yourself.

Our guard is lost again in pantomime.
Go ahead, shade the foreground whimsical.

I was ready for an awful rowing
but what flusters me is the dawdling.

Another stoppage to speed things up—
our work still synthetic,

and we remain unfixed in a robust
I hope not prideful way.

Then, at the post-mort,
from an orange water cooler

they pull pie from the sky
and slosh some out to us.

I just hope my hair will part.

The Pond

You skip enough stones the pond becomes a pile of stones.

That's the hovercraft we don't see.
That's the divine bannister.

The leaf pile morphs into a groundhog.
The groundhog into catastrophe.

It's been morning all along.

We're all pretending you don't have a disorder.

A Tree

As if love were weather were sorcery,
there's a tree, fallen, spread,
alive impossible
across the trickling Fort River,
a tall branch reaching up
the improvised trunk,
this doodle in everyday pining.

A Year

For a year now, no great intoxication of feeling,
just a weekly stumble into gibberish,

just our road, Rocky Hill,
the same in this town and the next,

and the next,
and the lilacs that cheat

nausea in our spring
that won't subdue the winter.

If I were a chord you pulled tension across—
How's that for a wish?—

on library days,
when sentiment seems suspect

and my greeting equals this ocean-sounds
noise-machine.

Different pavement,
we'd call the town differently.

Different shade,

we'd see invisible things.

Then, when it's time to go,
we can tip the couch out the second story window,

and if I drag it to the curb
it'll make a rowdy tribute.

Beta Blockers

Just one, and the swarm

in my chest
goes slow and quivering

like setting pudding
and in the aftereffect

I view myself
from a numb cheek of myself

capable of saying anything
whether or not I thought about it

and I suppose
relatively undamaged by dark meat

if you can believe it.

That is how they do, I guess, over at Wellness Center.

You've got to pay the meter.
You get fitted for a pair of try-out glasses.

The shot smarts. The orderly has a cold, a frown,

carries umbrage in his bosom.

This about sums up my problem with enthusiasm.

I note an effervescence and gear my toe toward its kickstand.

Some friends are saddened by this —

They wave their hands
like in their sleeves

are perfect-wrought elegies.

They start to apologize for what they can't control, like cars.

Membership Dwindles

You never know what'll happen
or who'll happen to be talking about it
on this park bench that doubles as a handrail

in our town so thoughtfully designed
around seating places.

Hard to say what was or wasn't apparent at the altar,
who was or wasn't snickering in his Polo
just below the membrane of reference.

Me, I try to be mantra-less,
to move through the day without beat,

without belief, and with little attention to luck,
in service of happenstance,
but not overly aroused by it—

A duty that is self-effacing.

The Fog

The one rule
is to lead with your yes,
but I'm still hung-up
half-out on the edge of the glade
with lots of un-reconciled mini-selves
unwilling to coalesce,
not about to leap together
into the giant Power Ranger.

Casual Forgetting

Dawn's crosstalk
is printed for us
in lavender today.

Otherwise you'll find it standard issue,
like loves one collects—

how through experience
you start to guess the wrap-up,

and a flirtation trends less naughty than before;
differently, too, with the channels unscrambled.

Please know I rose this morning
with the compulsion to clothe myself in binder clips,

to clip-in for a productive day,
get my dollar in its most unusual origami shape.

As a seashell regards the shore
and grows circumspect,

a little shrewd in the calculus
of making one's dimple there.

How Long Asleep in the Thought Cave?

Grandly inquisitive even of myself
as all summer we greeted winter's solving
in the nature camp where we abide,
the painted slab for hiding keys
abandoned
so you stub it.

Have you considered the statue was made to spin?—
with the summer light just right
and longest, summer like tautology,
while meanwhile the stone path
gets a lizard carved right into it.

Doesn't that sound good?
You foreigner collecting specimens
in the local circum-speak,
but that's how the town keeps track of itself—
as if one hauled a string of questions
and could throw them,

as if he could toss them out, hook a thing,
and call it back…

When I was called back…

I would cover you just like a bomb.

Might we find noticing preferable to looking-after?
Then, run to the dock and back again
and then begin to thunderstorm,

make purchase as if a powerful crystal,
uphill to do our gazing,
and let the bank account dwindle a bit,
let our hard-earned fold in on itself,
fold like icecream.

Or, never mind…

An innertube I rented once
from an outfit named
St. Mattress by the Springs
with which to float Deep Creek.

Luddite Dream

For a while we called it Netter Web,

and then, after that brief rhetorical rebellion
mostly went on over…

But all this time I've persisted in a small,
silent innovation: Webber Net.

How about you?

Analog

It was exciting to make a baby.
Little embryo we could not control.

How deep it grew inside you,
and distressing if it didn't divide right,

if allergy meds misplaced its penis,
making it the perfect thing to obsess about,

for like 14 hours / day,
somewhat replacing the old worry

with the dog's lazy hips,
the breed's troubling history with hips.

Landmarks at Night

Not on the road with the tree you can drive through

that fronts the museum
that sells the postcard
of the auto made of log,

which you don't purchase for a quarter
and send off again somewhere else.

Not headed toward the world's largest yarn ball,

nor at the feet of an art-deco Jesus six stories tall
tending his flock, The Ozarks,

yourself not in route to a sunny conference on tender adolescence,

nor rendered through a call-box
as a visiting neighbor bids his friend
please to buzz him up...

no six pack of cold ones to split...
no travel
none of that...

Just the dark
slender as a closing door.

Just the half-dark
cut with a nothing
that must be not-dark,
and is made easy
by the simple process of expecting it,
by chopping it into parts...

Then, the darker dark
the starting dark,

the dark with its starter's pomp,

dark walls that house you
that you softly punch.

If You Love It...

Do you remember the filmmaker who believed not in modern art
even as he filmed it,

believed not in psychoanalysis
as he inscribed himself on the fattest narratives,

as his films likely function as his own best shadow
of himself?

The moon mooning over him.

The moon with its man in it
as per usual over the pointed houses...

The moon in that way aspirant.

In the dark with its innumerable buzzing…
In our duplex by the power lines…

As somewhere a musical score
runs down the serendipity of everyday life…

As you put your finger to the flashlight
to make appearance of lewd shadows…

With the trees nevertheless on their whisper campaign…

When a correspondent sat bored at the kitchen table…

When a potted palm thrived all January in the south-facing window…

Or, when a little love sneaks up
and pinches from the passenger seat,

not really very seriously and not particularly meditatively,
not really in a classical way nor overly newfangled.

As in, one technique for handling persistence
is a constant recalculation of persistence.

One is whitewater rafting.

And strangely, sadly, I start to find things provincial and quaint
when I venture out from my New England

in this winter of broom snow
in the anyhoo philosophy of anything-ism

wherein belief is a mental trigger
that sublimates belief in concept

for belief in things
which is an ecclesiastical way of being.

I could praise a blender!
or a breakfast nook…

How we sat at the granite countertop…

If you love it so much why won't you fuck it up?

Why not make abode in the one cascading blip
referenced generally in literature as the orgasm?

and the layer that layers the habitat
and drive your Subaru over that?

As again one brings Twisted Tea to the Pinot Noir party
and another finds a door painted only a smidgen earlier

and in this stage stand boldly naked
and smear oneself with moisture cream

and give all the carpeting over to the puppy!

When there was never more a stranger than one's own husband…
When was he sprawled more ever than on this braided rug?

Always the new and turns out we could bare to look at it,

the carbonite building blocks
not teaching anything not adding up,

the crocus not obliged
not in time to be plucked up.

The guy we met who kept saying, Take me to your quarterback.

As in, one occupation is to go up and look about
and another to lie down in a field

and a third to sniff around
and its companion compulsion to take a sip

in the orgasm referenced generally as literature…

Excuse me, but I laughed every time, recorded everything
my friends and I, never once stopping to consider
our own self-importance. Now look at us,
in flight from ourselves, hyped up on one over-salient response.
That life robbed of particulars. When you were threadbare.
When the radio did a birdcall imitation of you
especially for you. In the time of throwing important things out…
The time we painted two walls the really green green of baseball,
decided this was the phase of basking around in it
and they made an algorithm of our personal tastes.
(How a collector of cards
stems also from the archetype of the failed counter of them.)
And someone else to think how smart that was.
Someone else to smooth the hitches.
I can't even get into how in love I was with my child.
What else might send one through such a dangerous loop of crying?
What else except maybe March Madness?

And the mountains turn blue again
on my Coors Light pint glass

in the fine variations of lower temperatures
when my neighbor nods to me
simply to say, "It's cold, Neighbor."

We had a mouse in the house…

Where's my Cascadian Farm Organic Cereal that is USDA Organic?

As a thing that happens enough may cease to exist…

As one who misspells the word "positive" may for a moment
consider himself the invented superhero Positron

and summarily learn easily to make lentils in the slow cooker.

Or, when a little love catches one
all mystical on the couch cushion…

To this thing and to that saying, You are not my lover…

When a little blasphemy carouses around…
When the blaspheme is myself

and disbelief the simultaneous
companion and container of me…

And the point guard knows the Zen of college basketball.
And the table lamp how many shells piled within it.

I could praise a power wire!
or a turn signal

from my solace space on the three-season porch,
on the nightiest night of the season to date,

whispering,

    If art is saying a thing the weird way
    then love is never shirking from it.

Acknowledgements

Joyful thanks to my family and friends for their love and support.

Thank you David Bartone, Luke Bloomfield, Jeff Downey, Rachel Glaser, Anne Holmes, Emily Hunt, Greg Lawless, Kelin Loe, Carlin Mackie, Dara Wier, and Mike Young for your insight and assistance with these poems.

Thank you especially Arda Collins and members of the Flying Object manuscript group.

Deepest gratitude to Richard Dillard.

Grateful acknowledgement to the editors of the following periodicals in which some of these poems first appeared: *H_ngm_n, Pangyrus, Sink Review, Spoke Too Soon, Sprung Formal,* and on the *Verse* website.

This book was designed and set in Palatino Linotype by RHWD Industries

Cover photograph by Emily Hunt

Photograph of the author by Liane Malinowski

Printed by Salem Printing

groundhog
POETRY PRESS